D1274419

Nuclear Energy

Robert Snedden

Heinemann Library
Chicago, Illinois

Text and cover designed by Celia Floyd
Illustrated by Jeff Edwards and Alan Fraser

Originated by Ambassador Litho Ltd.
Printed in Hong Kong by Wing King Tong

06 05 04 03 02
10 9 8 7 6 5 4 3 2 1

Library of Congress Cataloging-in-Publication Data
Snedden, Robert.
  Nuclear energy / by Robert Snedden.
      p. cm. -- (Essential energy)
Includes bibliographical references and index.
  ISBN 1-57572-444-8 (lib. bdg.)
  1. Nuclear energy--Juvenile literature. [1. Nuclear energy.] I.
Title.
  QC792.5 .S54 2001
  333.792'4--dc21
                                            00-013239

Acknowledgments
The author and publishers are grateful to the following for permission to reproduce copyright material:
Environmental Images: pp.4, 22, 24, 30, 31, 36; Corbis: pp.5, 11, 14, 28; Science Photo Library: pp.8,
12, 15, 17, 20, 23, 25, 26, 27, 29, 32, 33, 37, 41; Camera Press: p.13; Robert Harding Picture Library:
p.18; Landauer: p.34; Popperfoto: pp.39, 42, 43.

Cover photograph reproduced with permission of Robert Harding Picture Library.

Every effort has been made to contact copyright holders of any material reproduced in this book. Any
omissions will be rectified in subsequent printings if notice is given to the publisher.

Some words are shown in bold, **like this.** You can find out what they
mean by looking in the glossary.

Contents

Nuclear Power? No Thanks?

At the beginning of the 1900s, no one dreamed that there could be such a thing as nuclear power. Scientists were just beginning to discover **radioactivity** and taking their first steps toward discovering how **atoms,** the particles from which all matter is made, are put together. In 1905, Albert Einstein showed that **mass** could be changed into energy, and vice versa. By 1918, Sir Ernest Rutherford had shown that atoms could be split. By 1942, the world had its first nuclear **reactor.**

By the 1990s, nuclear power had become the second-biggest source of energy for the industrialized world. **Fossil fuels** are still the top source of energy today. For many people, **nuclear energy** was the answer to the problem of dwindling fossil fuel resources and the pollution caused by burning fossil fuels. However, the nuclear industry has stopped growing. Few countries are building new reactors. Germany, for example, announced in June 2000 that it would stop using all its nuclear power plants. Why are people turning away from nuclear power?

Protesters demonstrated for a month against the Superphénix nuclear reactor in France.

Reactor reactions

Many people are concerned about the environmental and health problems linked to nuclear power. Nuclear reactors produce **radiation,** which is harmful to living things. However, with or without nuclear power, radiation is a fact of life. It comes from the Sun, from rocks, from medical X-rays, and even from television sets. High doses of radiation can kill very quickly. Small doses, such as what might leak from a normally operating nuclear plant, could build up over many years and cause damage. Some scientists estimate that the average person gets five times as much radiation in a lifetime from sitting in front of the television or a computer monitor as he or she would from living near a nuclear power station.

Nuclear power is also seen as a problem because of its connection to nuclear weapons. Accidents, such as fires or explosions, could cause **radioactive** materials to be given off inside the power station, or even outside. Government regulators in the United States have estimated that there is about a 50 percent chance of a core **meltdown** in a U.S. reactor within any 20-year period. Disposing of the dangerous waste that is the by-product of nuclear power is also a problem.

Many people are afraid of nuclear reactors due to the possibility of accidents.

Inside the Atom

To understand how nuclear power works, we first have to consider how **atoms** are put together. Atoms are the tiny particles from which all materials are made. An atom can be divided into two parts. The first part is an outer cloud of tiny particles called **electrons.** The number of electrons in the outermost part of this cloud determines how the atom will react with other atoms in chemical reactions.

The second part of the atom is its inner part—the **nucleus.** The nucleus is made up of a tightly-packed cluster of particles called **protons** and **neutrons.** Each **element** has a different number of protons and neutrons. Elements range in complexity from hydrogen, the simplest element, which has a single proton, to uranium, which is used as a nuclear fuel and can have 235 or more protons and neutrons. Some elements can have even more particles in their nuclei. The atoms of a particular element all have the same number of protons in their nuclei. This number is called the **atomic number.** The protons and neutrons take no part in chemical reactions—only the electrons do.

The central nucleus of an atom, which is made up of a cluster of protons and neutrons, is surrounded by orbiting electrons.

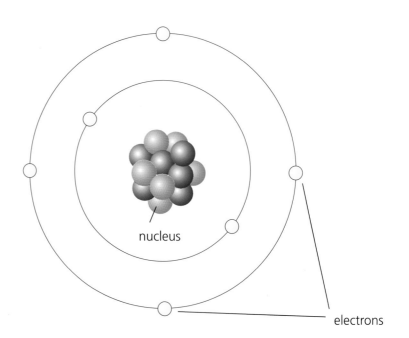

nucleus

electrons

Radioactive elements

A **radioactive** substance is one in which the nuclei of its atoms are unstable. They break apart, giving out energy as they do so. When the nucleus **decays,** some of its **mass** is changed to energy, which is then given off as a particle, or **photon,** of **radiation.** A radioactive element may go through several stages of decay before finally becoming a stable element.

Of the 112 known elements, 92 occur in nature. These elements have atomic numbers ranging from 1 (hydrogen) to 92 (uranium). Of these elements, 81 are stable; all the others are radioactive. The radioactive elements include technetium, which is number 43; promethium, number 61; and all the elements from polonium, number 84, up to uranium, number 92.

Isotopes

It is possible for two or more atoms to have the same atomic number, but different numbers of neutrons. These atoms are the same element, but are called **isotopes** of that element. Isotopes may be stable, which means that their nucleus cannot change its composition. Or they can be radioactive, which means that their nucleus can change its composition. Elements can be part of nature or made in a laboratory. For example, carbon (C) has the isotopes C12, which is stable, and C14, which is radioactive. The name *C12* means that it is a carbon with 12 neutrons. C14 has 14 neutrons.

Half-life

There is no way to predict when a radioactive nucleus will complete the decaying process. But scientists have used observations and mathematics to learn how long it takes half of the atoms in a radioactive sample to decay. This is called the radioactive element's **half-life.** Each radioactive isotope has a different half-life. These can range from a tiny fraction of a second to billions of years. The half-life of polonium 213 is about four millionths of a second. The half-life of uranium 238 is about the same as the age of Earth, 4.5 billion years.

Energy from the Atom

An **element** is a substance that cannot be split chemically into simpler substances. Elements can react together in chemical reactions. All chemical reactions involve the giving off or the taking up of **chemical energy.** For instance, when coal is burned, the carbon in the coal combines with oxygen to become carbon dioxide, and energy is given off as heat. The **atoms** involved in a chemical reaction remain unchanged.

In contrast, the elements involved in a nuclear reaction can change as a result of it. In a nuclear reaction, an unstable atomic **nucleus decays.** As it does so, it gives off **radiation** in the form of particles or **photons.** A large, unstable nucleus can also give off **neutrons** as it decays.

Missing mass

No **mass** is ever lost when a chemical reaction takes place. The mass of the atoms present before the reaction will always equal the mass of those after the reaction. However, if you add up the mass of all the particles formed by the decay of an unstable nucleus, you will find that it is less than the mass of the original nucleus. So where is the missing mass?

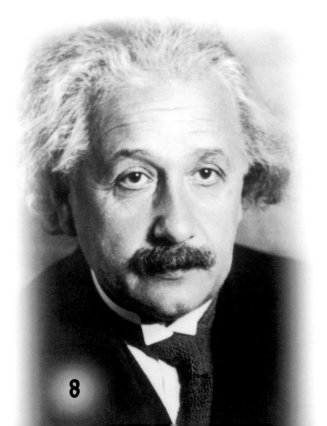

$E = mc^2$

As part of his famous theory of relativity, Albert Einstein showed that mass (m) and energy (E) were related by the equation $E = mc^2$, where c = the speed of light. In a nuclear reaction, mass is changed into energy. For example, the Sun produces a huge amount of energy from nuclear reactions in its core that change hydrogen into helium. In the process, the Sun loses four million tons of mass every second!

In his theory of relativity, Albert Einstein (1879–1955) revealed the connection between matter and energy.

When a nucleus decays, energy is given off. The amount of energy given off is very large. A given mass of uranium can provide 2.5 million times more energy than would result from burning the same mass of carbon.

Most of the energy is in the form of **kinetic energy** as the nucleus breaks apart. This kinetic energy is rapidly changed into **heat energy** as the fragments of the nucleus collide with other atoms. It is this heat that is used to generate electricity in a nuclear power station. Some of the remaining energy is carried off as radiation.

Radioactive decay

When the nucleus of a **radioactive** element breaks down, it can give off different types of radiation.

- **alpha particles** (α) are made up of two **protons** and two neutrons. They are fast moving but can be stopped by a sheet of paper and will not travel far through the air.
- **beta particles** (β) are fast-moving **electrons.** They are more difficult to stop than alpha particles but can be stopped by a thin sheet of metal.
- gamma rays (γ) are not particles; they are a form of electromagnetic radiation with a very short wavelength and a lot of energy. **Gamma radiation** is not easy to stop—a thick sheet of lead is needed to block gamma rays.

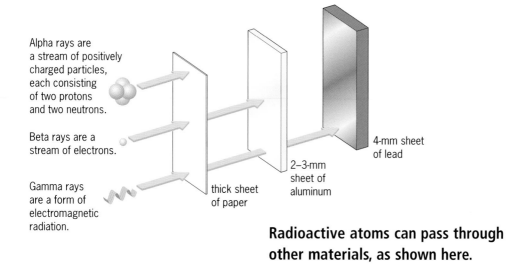

Alpha rays are a stream of positively charged particles, each consisting of two protons and two neutrons.

Beta rays are a stream of electrons.

Gamma rays are a form of electromagnetic radiation.

thick sheet of paper

2–3-mm sheet of aluminum

4-mm sheet of lead

Radioactive atoms can pass through other materials, as shown here.

Neutrons and Chain Reactions

Naturally occurring uranium (U) contains two **isotopes**, U238 and U235. Uranium 235 is a **fissile material**. This means that if a U235 **nucleus** is struck by a **neutron**, it will **fission**, or break apart. Neutrons striking U238 nuclei will simply be scattered. As the U235 nucleus breaks apart, it gives off energy and two or three more neutrons. These neutrons travel at around 12,430 miles (20,000 kilometers) per second. That is about 25,000 times faster than a space shuttle orbiting Earth! Because these neutrons can set off a **chain reaction**, they make it possible to get a continuous supply of energy from uranium.

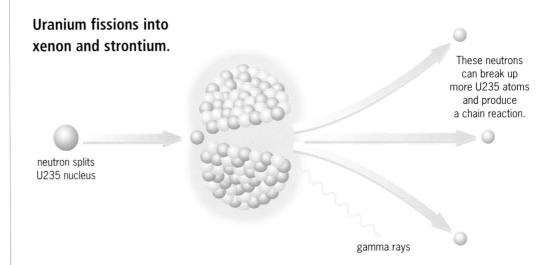

Uranium fissions into xenon and strontium.

neutron splits
U235 nucleus

These neutrons can break up more U235 atoms and produce a chain reaction.

gamma rays

Chain reactions

In a chain reaction, the neutrons given off by the fissioning uranium strike other nuclei. When they strike U235 nuclei, these fission, too, releasing still more neutrons. These neutrons can go on to strike yet more nuclei, which give off yet more neutrons, and so on. To increase the chances of neutrons striking U235, scientists working in nuclear power stations enrich the uranium by adding more U235 to each sample.

There is no single chain reaction taking place. Within a typical nuclear power station there may be about 100 million billion fission chain reactions taking place at any time.

The new nuclei formed when an unstable nucleus **decays** are called fission products. These new **atoms** are also unstable and will decay further.

The amount of power produced by a **reactor** can be increased or decreased by controlling the chain reactions. If materials that absorb neutrons are put into the reactor, there will be fewer neutrons moving around and fewer fissions. **Boron** is such a material. Nuclear reactors use control rods that contain boron carbide to control power output.

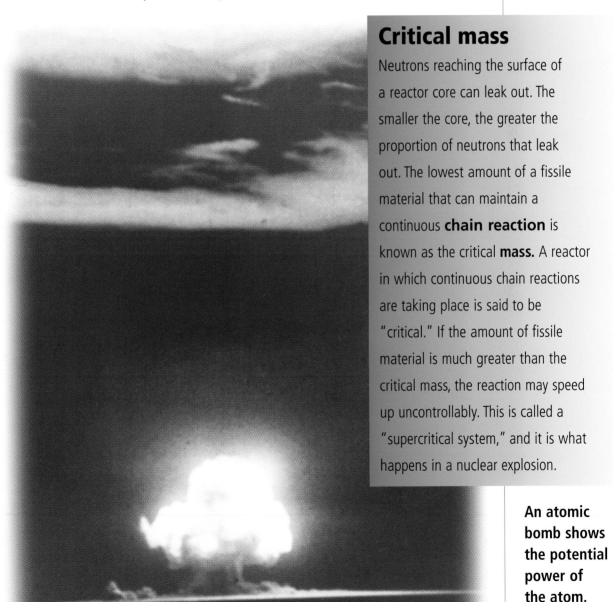

Critical mass

Neutrons reaching the surface of a reactor core can leak out. The smaller the core, the greater the proportion of neutrons that leak out. The lowest amount of a fissile material that can maintain a continuous **chain reaction** is known as the critical **mass.** A reactor in which continuous chain reactions are taking place is said to be "critical." If the amount of fissile material is much greater than the critical mass, the reaction may speed up uncontrollably. This is called a "supercritical system," and it is what happens in a nuclear explosion.

An atomic bomb shows the potential power of the atom.

Unlocking the Atom

During the early 1900s, many researchers were investigating what happens when **neutrons** strike uranium **atoms.** In 1938, German scientists Otto Hahn and Fritz Strassmann showed that when uranium is bombarded with neutrons, new, lighter **elements** are formed. A year later, Lise Meitner and Otto Frisch started using the word *fission* to describe this process.

Developing weapons

The outbreak of World War II (1939–1945) led people to explore the uses of fission as a source of energy, especially in the creation of weapons. Developing a weapon required not only a continuous fission reaction but also enough fissionable material to use in a weapon.

The U.S. government poured a large amount of money and resources into a nuclear research team called the Manhattan Project. Another team, led by Enrico Fermi, soon succeeded in making the first self-sustaining nuclear **reactor** on December 2, 1942. Work for the Manhattan Project, which built on Fermi's success, took place in Tennessee, Washington, California, and New Mexico.

The world's second nuclear reactor was built at the Argonne Forest Laboratory in Chicago, Illinois, in 1943.

As we have seen, only the U235 **isotope** fissions, and natural uranium only contains 0.7 percent of U235. To make a bomb, much higher concentrations of U235 are necessary. Part of the Manhattan Project's aim was to develop a way of separating U235 from U238. The solution was gas diffusion.

Another way to develop weapons is to use a different fissile **nucleus.** When Uranium 238 reacts with neutrons, it forms U239. The U239 then **decays** in two steps to form Plutonium 239. This Pu239 can be used in the manufacture of weapons. Once Fermi had demonstrated that a reactor could be built, the focus turned to building reactors to produce plutonium. The first such reactor was constructed in Oak Ridge, Tennessee. It took less than three years to develop this entirely new technology, which prepared the way for developing **nuclear energy** for public use.

Atoms for Peace

The Atomic Energy Commission was set up in 1946 to oversee nonmilitary uses of nuclear power in the United States. In December 1953, in a speech at the United Nations, U. S. President Dwight D. Eisenhower announced his decision to make nuclear-related information available to other countries in order to develop peaceful applications for nuclear energy. He called his program "atoms for peace." The first international conference on nuclear energy was held in Geneva, Switzerland, in 1955. The first Soviet nuclear power plant began operations in 1954. Britain began production of nuclear-fueled electricity in 1956. The French began building their first commercial plants in 1957. By the early 1960s, nuclear power was firmly established as a commercial energy source.

President Eisenhower supported the use of nuclear power for peaceful, domestic uses, such as the production of electricity.

Uranium Mining

The first stage in the nuclear fuel process is mining the uranium ore, the rock in which uranium is found. Uranium is one of the less common **elements,** although it is about twenty times more common than precious metals such as silver. Mining takes place at locations where the concentration of uranium is greater than about 0.04 percent of each rock sample. Below this amount, it would cost too much to remove the uranium.

Uranium is usually found as uraninite, an **oxide** of uranium. The uranium is separated by first crushing the rock and then treating it with chemicals. The uranium leaves the mine as "yellowcake," or uranium concentrate, another oxide of uranium. Because the uranium concentrations are generally very low, a lot of waste is produced when uranium is removed from its ore. Even ore that is considered to have a high concentration will be made up of only about one percent uranium.

How much uranium?

Like **fossil fuels,** uranium is a nonrenewable resource. There is only a limited amount available. However, how long it will last is influenced by a number of factors. If nuclear power is gradually phased out, the use of uranium will decline, and the reserves will last much longer. Another possibility is that the uranium currently stored in nuclear weapons could become available for power generation if these weapons were taken out of use.

This uranium mine is in Australia.

The risks of mining

Uranium is **radioactive,** and **radiation** poses health risks for people exposed to high levels of it. All of the different **isotopes** that uranium forms as it **decays** are present in the ore. Because these are different elements, they will be chemically different from uranium and so will form part of the waste material. The waste products left behind after the uranium has been removed can be buried to lower the risk of exposing anyone to radiation.

One of these wastes is a radioactive isotope of the gas radon. This element is given off from the waste material. If radon is inhaled, it can cause damage to the inside of the lungs. In underground uranium mines, the radon tends to accumulate. This makes the mine unsafe for the miners who work there.

Cutting the risks, raising the costs

Miners exposed to the average dose of **radiation** in a mine are six times more likely to develop lung cancer than other people. An American group called the Union of Concerned Scientists says that radon levels can be lowered simply by allowing more air into the mines. The group estimated that the cost of bringing exposure down to reasonably safe levels would be between ten and twenty percent of the value of the uranium mined.

Unfortunately, spending money to do this would cut down the amount of money the mine would make, unless the mine owner raised the selling price of the uranium the mine produced. Power stations buy their uranium from the cheapest source they can find. Because of this, they discourage mines from taking steps to increase safety. For many miners, working in mines may be risky, but is better than no work at all.

The fuel used in nuclear **reactors** is uranium 235, shown here.

Producing Nuclear Fuels

Yellowcake is the raw material for nuclear fuel production. The uranium in the yellowcake is not pure. The first part of the process changes the yellowcake to a pure orange-yellow powder. Next, the powder is heated in a stream of hydrogen gas at a temperature of 1,200° F (650° C). This produces chocolate-brown uranium dioxide. Some types of **reactors** can use uranium in this form as a fuel, but most use uranium dioxide that has been enriched to contain a higher proportion of U235 than U238.

Enriching uranium

There are two ways to enrich uranium. In both methods, the process begins by heating the uranium dioxide. First, it is heated with hydrogen fluoride gas. The product of that process, uranium hexaflouride gas, is then heated in fluorine gas, which still contains U235 and U238 **atoms.**

Gas diffusion enrichment

The lighter **molecules** of a gas will pass, or **diffuse,** through a **porous** material faster than the heavier molecules. In the gas diffusion enrichment method, the uranium hexafluoride gas is passed through a porous material. The molecules with the lighter U235 atoms diffuse faster than the molecules with U238. This is the most common uranium enrichment method in the United States, but it takes a long time. After one pass, the sample may be only 1.004 times richer in U235 than before. Gas diffusion uses a lot of energy. Another, preferred method of uranium enrichment is called gas centrifuge enrichment.

Fuel production risks

The biggest risks of nuclear fuel production come not from possible exposure to **radiation,** but from the chemicals used to process the fuel. Fluorine and hydrogen fluoride are extremely dangerous chemicals. Both flourine and hydrogen fluoride can cause severe burns if they come into contact with a person's skin. Hydrofluoric acid, which is a solution of hydrogen fluoride in water, moves deep into the skin tissues, but it may be several hours before pain develops and the destruction of the tissues begins.

This gas diffusion enrichment plant is in Paducah, Kentucky.

Gas centrifuge enrichment

Outside the United States, uranium is enriched using a method called gas centrifuge enrichment. In this process, uranium hexafluoride is spun in a cylinder at around 1,000 revolutions per second. Molecules containing U238 tend to move toward the wall of the container more readily. This leaves the lighter U235 molecules in the center. This is not a perfect method, however, because the gas molecules tend to mix again. However, gas removed from the center will be richer in U235. Once the uranium hexafluoride has been enriched, it is changed back into uranium dioxide by heating it with hydrogen and steam.

Gas centrifuge enrichment plants are smaller and less expensive to run than gas diffusion plants. However, the centrifuge equipment itself is very expensive, so it costs a lot of money to build a centrifuge enrichment plant. Companies are now finding ways to use lasers to enrich uranium for even less money.

Inside a Nuclear Power Station

Many of the features of a nuclear power station are similar to those of other power stations. A source of fuel, such as coal, gas, or oil in a **fossil fuel** station, is used to provide energy to heat water and produce high-energy steam to spin a **turbine.** The mechanical energy of the turbine is used to generate electricity. The steam is turned back into liquid water and recycled to the steam generator.

A worker changes fuel rods in a nuclear power station in Switzerland.

The reactor core

The heart of a nuclear power station is the **reactor** core. This is where the nuclear fuel is held and where it undergoes **fission** to produce energy. The fuel is in the form of a stack of pellets or a cylindrical rod held in a thin-walled metal container called **cladding.** The rods and cladding together are called **fuel rods.** In most reactors, a fuel **element** is made of several fuel rods bundled together with spaces between them through which liquid **coolants** can flow. There are 200 or more fuel elements in most reactors. A fuel element will produce energy for three to six years before it has to be replaced.

Coolants

The gas or liquid coolant passes through the reactor core and carries the heat away to the steam generators. The coolant comes into contact with the cladding, not directly with the nuclear fuel. A coolant has to be selected carefully. It must not react chemically with the cladding. It must not absorb too many **neutrons** because this would slow down the **chain reactions.** And, it should not be expensive. Most reactors use carbon dioxide, helium gases, and light and heavy water. Light water is ordinary everyday water; heavy water has an **isotope** of hydrogen in which the hydrogen **atom** has a neutron in its **nucleus** as well as a **proton.**

The heated gas is pumped to generators where steam is produced. If light water is used, it may be allowed to boil, producing steam directly. This is called a *direct steam cycle.* Otherwise, if heavy water is being used, it may be used to heat a separate water supply in what is called an *indirect steam cycle.* The coolant is pumped back to the reactor after it has been used to heat the steam.

Moderators

A **moderator** is a substance that slows down neutrons so they have a greater chance of striking fissile U235 nuclei. The moderator surrounds the fuel rods. It is generally a material such as graphite or heavy water.

Pressure vessels and shielding

The coolant in a nuclear reactor is kept under pressure. For this reason, the reactor core is surrounded by a pressure vessel. It is extremely important for the people working in a nuclear power plant to be shielded from harmful **radiation.** The pressure vessel gives some protection, but most reactors require an additional shield. This is called *the biological shield.* The shield has to be thick enough to protect the workers from neutrons and **gamma radiation** at all times. Concrete is a very good shielding material. Usually, a concrete shield about seven to ten feet (two to three meters) thick surrounds the reactor.

Control and Containment

Several steps are taken to make sure that **radioactive** materials stay inside the **reactor**. The **cladding** keeps the **fission** products in the **fuel rods,** but if they do escape, they will enter the **coolant.** The coolant flows around the reactor and is designed to keep fission products from escaping into the environment. If there is a leak in the coolant circuit, **radiation** will escape. However, there is another barrier that prevents radiation from spreading into the outside world. This next barrier is the building itself, which is why it is called a reactor containment building.

Reactor control

The **chain reactions** in a nuclear reactor can be controlled by placing materials that absorb **neutrons** inside the reactors. This is done by using control rods that contain a neutron absorber, such as **boron** or cadmium. These rods can be moved in and out of the reactor as necessary. If the reactor is critical, meaning there is a continuous series of chain reactions in progress, it can be shut down by introducing control rods. The reactor can be started up again by simply removing the rods. The control rods do not have to be actual rods of material. Some reactors use a neutron-absorbing liquid or gas in their shutdown system.

Nuclear reactor control rods are inserted into the reactor core to absorb neutrons and slow down the chain reactions.

A reactor usually has 50 or more control rods spread throughout its core. The operators of the power station regulate the output of the reactor by adjusting the positions of the rods. They move the rods in and out as the reactor is running to produce higher or lower levels of power output. The rate at which fission is taking place in the reactor core is

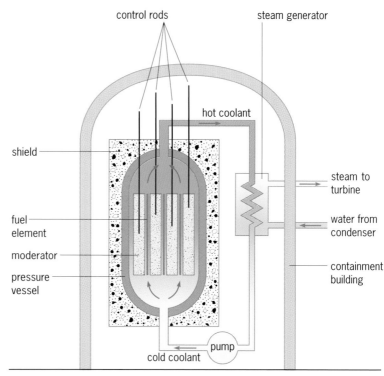

This diagram shows the different parts of a nuclear reactor.

determined by measuring the number of neutrons present in different parts of the reactor. The temperature and pressure of the coolant are also measured.

Shutdown rods

A reactor is also equipped with shutdown rods. These are absorbers that are kept out of the core when the reactor is running, or in the core when the reactor has been shut down. The shutdown rods are controlled independently and are used to stop the chain reactions rapidly during an emergency.

Fission product heating

Even when the reactor has been shut down, it will still continue to produce heat. The chain reaction can be stopped by using control rods, but there is no way to stop the natural breakdown of the **radioactive** materials. The heat produced by this breakdown is called fission product heating. If steps are not taken to remove this heat, the fuel may melt. It is essential that the reactor core is cooled at all times, even when it is not producing energy. Emergency core-cooling systems are kept ready in case the main cooling system fails.

Reactor Systems

There are several different types of nuclear power stations around the world. Here, we will look at the more common types of **reactors.**

Light water reactors (LWRs)

Almost all of the nuclear power plants in the United States are light water reactors. This type of reactor uses nuclear fuel in the form of uranium **oxide** enriched to about three percent U235. In light water reactors, the **moderator** and **coolant** are made of highly purified water.

Pressurized water reactors (PWRs)

One type of light water reactor is the pressurized water reactor. PWRs are the most commonly used reactors in the world. Like light water reactors, PWRs use normal water as both their coolant and their moderator. Because water absorbs **neutrons,** PWRs use enriched uranium.

Taking apart an AGR, an advanced gas-cooled reactor, is a lengthy and dangerous process.

The PWR uses uranium dioxide **fuel rods** coated with a zirconium alloy, which resists water damage and does not absorb neutrons. The core of a PWR reactor is smaller than that of an advanced gas-cooled reactor, known as an AGR. Some of the fuel rods are left out to make room for the control and shutdown rods, which move up and down within the fuel elements. The whole core is inside a steel pressure vessel eight inches (twenty centimeters) thick. PWRs give off about 3,000 megawatts of heat and 1,000 megawatts of electricity The PWR has no cooling channels and the fuel elements are packed closely together. Coolant has to be sent through the core between the fuel rods and then pumped to a steam generator. After transferring its heat, the coolant is pumped back to the reactor. Each reactor has three or four of these cooling cycles.

To maintain a constant coolant pressure there is a pressurizer, with a pressure-release valve in case the pressure gets too high. This is an essential part of the power station—if it goes wrong it can be disastrous. The reactor and the cooling systems are enclosed within a containment building with concrete walls about three feet (one meter) thick. This is necessary because if the cooling system burst open, the high-pressure water inside would turn to steam instantly. This would cause a huge increase in pressure inside the building that could break apart the walls.

Advanced gas-cooled reactors (AGRs)

Advanced gas-cooled reactors supply more than half the electricity produced by nuclear reactors in Britain. They use enriched uranium dioxide as their fuel. AGRs use gas, specifically carbon dioxide, as their coolant. The core of an AGR is made from blocks of graphite through which cylindrical cooling channels are cut. The fuel elements are placed in these channels and coolant flows through the channels. The heat output of an AGR is around 1,500 megawatts. From this, it produces 600 megawatts of electricity, making it about 40 percent efficient. This output is similar to that of a **fossil fuel** power station.

The pressure vessel is made of special concrete around thirteen to twenty feet (four to six meters) thick, with a thin lining of stainless steel to keep the coolant gas from escaping. After heating, the coolant gas is pumped to the steam generators, which are set in the walls of the concrete pressure vessel. Once the steam has been generated, the coolant is recycled to the reactor core. The steam produced goes to a steam **turbine,** where electricity is produced.

This PWR station is in Palo Verde, California.

Fast Breeders, Fast Movers

Fast breeder **reactors** are used to produce new **fissile material** in the form of plutonium. A fast breeder reactor actually produces more fuel than it uses. This is possible because when uranium 238 absorbs a **neutron** during the operation of a reactor, it is changed into plutonium 239, which is an **isotope** that can be **fissioned** and can be used to fuel reactors.

A typical breeder reactor has a large inner core, which is made up of a large number of stainless-steel tubes filled with a mixture of uranium **oxide** and plutonium oxide. The core is surrounded by an outer blanket of tubes of natural uranium oxide. This captures neutrons that escape from the core, and the uranium is changed into plutonium. As in other reactors, heat is removed from the core by a liquid **coolant** and is used to produce steam, which powers a **turbine** that drives an electrical generator.

The core of a fast breeder reactor is very small because it has no **moderator.** A core 8 feet (2.5 meters) in diameter and 5 feet (1.5 meters) high will produce 1,000 megawatts of electricity. It also produces a great deal of heat—about three and a half times that of a pressurized water reactor. Liquid sodium is commonly used as a coolant. This substance transfers heat efficiently and, unlike water, does not readily absorb neutrons. The **heat energy** produced by the reactor core is so high that the fuel would melt in seconds if the coolant stopped flowing for any reason. As extra protection, the whole core is placed in a pool of liquid sodium into which heat can pass if the coolant system fails.

This is the reactor room at the Beloyarskaya fast breeder in Russia.

This experimental fast breeder reactor is west of Idaho Falls, Idaho.

Shutdowns

The world's first fast breeder in public use was the Superphénix, built in France. It began to produce electricity in 1986 but has had many shutdowns since then. The technology is protested by many people.

In the United States, where many people are worried about the effect of plutonium on the environment or the danger that plutonium might fall into the hands of **terrorists,** breeder reactors are no longer being developed. Congress stopped funding breeder technology in 1983. Britain shut down its first breeder reactor in 1994. In December 1995, Japan's breeder reactor, Monju, had a broken pipe that spilled about two to five tons of liquid sodium. The sodium then caught fire. The reactor is located 2,300 feet (700 meters) from an active earthquake fault.

Nuclear energy on the move

The U.S. Navy recognized the potential of nuclear power as an energy source. A program to develop a naval reactor was launched during the late 1940s. In 1954, the first nuclear submarine, the Nautilus, was launched. It was a complete success. Today, many of the world's navies use nuclear-powered submarines.

The Nautilus reactor was the prototype for the first American commercial nuclear power plant, which was built in Shippingport, Pennsylvania, in 1957. The U.S.S. Triton, which was launched in 1959, was propelled by two nuclear reactors. In 1960, the submarine traveled around the world underwater, covering 49,000 miles (78,858 kilometers) in 84 days.

Spent Fuel and Reprocessing

Nuclear fuel lasts for about six years in a **reactor.** After it is removed, it is called spent fuel. This spent fuel is made up of uranium, different **isotopes** of plutonium, and some different **fission products.** It is extremely dangerous because it is about 100 million times more **radioactive** than fresh fuel. Most of this **radioactivity** is due to the fission products which are themselves **decaying** and giving off **radiation.** There are two ways to deal with the spent fuel. It can be either stored or reprocessed.

Reprocessing

After spent fuel is removed from the reactor, it is stored in 33-foot (10-meter) deep water ponds on the reactor site. The spent fuel is kept here for a year or so to allow some of the shorter-lived fission products to decay. This makes it slightly less dangerous for the workers who will handle it later. The water also cools the fuel. Some fission products leak through holes in the **cladding** and **contaminate** the water, so the water itself becomes a low-level waste that needs to be disposed of. The spent fuel then has to be brought to a reprocessing plant. Many

people question the safety of the flasks that are used to transport the fuel from reactor sites to reprocessing plants. In one test, a flask was placed in front of a 140-ton locomotive that was traveling at a speed of 100 miles (160 kilometers) per hour. Despite the collision, the flask remained intact.

A flask for transporting spent nuclear fuel sits on a railway carriage.

The first stage in reprocessing spent fuel is to chop up the **fuel rods** and dissolve them in nitric acid. This gives off gas fission products, some of which have to be collected and disposed of. These substances, plus the fuel cladding, become an intermediate, or medium-level, waste disposal problem.

The next stage is the separation of the uranium and plutonium from the fission products. A solution of the fission products then has to be stored as high-level waste. The uranium and plutonium are then separated from each other. Nearly all of this material is stored. If uranium were to become scarce, it could be used for reactor fuel at some point in the future.

Reprocessing and nuclear weapons

Reprocessing is the link between nuclear reactors and nuclear weapons because it provides the plutonium for the manufacture of weapons. The United States banned commercial fuel reprocessing during the 1970s.

These storage cylinders contain uranium 238 removed during the process of enriching uranium for nuclear fuel.

Dealing with Nuclear Waste

One of the biggest challenges for the nuclear industry is the question of what to do with **radioactive** waste. Low-level nuclear waste is made up of materials such as **contaminated** clothing, packing material, and fittings from nuclear **reactors.** Intermediate-level wastes include fuel **cladding** and wastes from fuel reprocessing. Intermediate-level wastes require more careful storage than low-level wastes.

Low-level nuclear wastes are placed in concrete-lined trenches and covered with soil at waste sites. Despite protests, some liquid low-level wastes have simply been pumped into the ocean.

High-level waste disposal

High-level waste includes spent **fuel rods** and **fission products** such as plutonium. Spent fuel produces so much heat that it has to be cooled for decades and requires elaborate storage.

Disposing of wastes is different from storing them. Stored wastes are kept safe and accessible for up to 100 years, in case they need to be used in the future. Disposing of wastes means putting them safely out of reach with no plans for their recovery. The current preference is to dispose of high-level waste by burying it in deep underground tunnels.

Spent nuclear fuel is encased in glass in a reprocessing plant.

First the waste is encased in a highly resistant glass. Next, cylinders of the encased waste are placed in 10-inch (25-centimeter) thick stainless steel containers. These containers can then be placed in underground shafts and tunnels between 985 to 3,280 feet (300 to 1,000 meters) deep. The tunnels are then backfilled with clay and other materials that prevent water from getting at the containers. The tunnel walls may also be lined with concrete as a further barrier. The final barrier is the hundreds of yards of rock between the tunnels and the surface.

The U.S. government plans to build a nuclear waste depository in Yucca Mountain, Nevada, shown here.

Eventually, nuclear power stations might simply become facilities for holding nuclear waste. The U.S. Department of Energy was required to begin accepting spent nuclear fuel for disposal in January 1998, but it will be at least 2010 before its fuel burial site in Yucca Mountain, Nevada, is ready.

Storing radioactive wastes

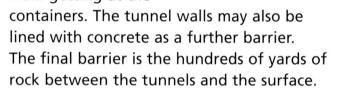

It is very difficult to say how quickly radioactive wastes **decay**. There will be a range of different radioactive **isotopes** present, each with a different **half-life,** and each decaying into new radioactive isotopes which themselves will have different half-lives. The decay rate continues at a fast pace for between 100 and 1,000 years after the radioactive waste was formed. After that, the rate slows. Spent fuel has to be kept cooled for decades until the shorter half-life isotopes have decayed, and must be kept out of contact with the rest of the environment for hundreds of years.

Disposal Dilemma

A major problem in disposing of nuclear waste lies in finding a suitable site. Most people do not want to live near a waste dump, especially a waste dump containing harmful materials. No matter how much the industry or government might argue that the waste is safely locked away, people would still object.

A train-load of nuclear waste on its way to a disposal site passes the village of Seascale in Great Britain.

Can we be certain?

Can scientists ever say with absolute certainty that a waste disposal site will remain secure over thousands of years? Most likely, no. Nuclear waste has to be kept away from people and the environment for 1,000 years at the very least. Furthermore, it is very difficult to predict how conditions will change over such a long period. This makes rating potential waste sites extremely difficult. For small countries with large numbers of people, there may be no acceptable sites for high-level waste disposal. Many people believe that there is no effective solution to the problem of nuclear waste.

A wider problem

Nuclear waste disposal is by no means the only disposal problem we have to face. We are rapidly running out of places to put new landfill sites for the millions of tons of household and industrial waste we create. Many people believe that the carbon dioxide waste given off by **fossil fuel** power stations into the atmosphere is leading to global climate changes. We need to find ways to better manage dangerous wastes of all kinds.

To reprocess or not to reprocess?

Reprocessing nuclear waste actually creates an even larger volume of waste to be disposed of. An advantage of reprocessing nuclear waste is that it concentrates the dangerous high-level waste into a small volume. However, a major disadvantage is the large amount of separated plutonium that it produces. When plutonium was going to be an important part of breeder **reactors,** there was a reason for reprocessing nuclear waste. However, this is no longer the case. Most fast-breeder programs have been cut back, delayed, or canceled. For many people, the risks involved with reprocessing nuclear waste are a strong argument against it and the long-term storage of spent fuel.

Waste production

At each stage of reprocessing, wastes are produced. From the reprocessing of 5.2 cubic yards (4 cubic meters) of spent fuel from a typical pressurized water reactor, or PWR, 3.3 cubic yards (2.5 cubic meters) of high-level waste, 52 cubic yards (40 cubic meters) of intermediate-level waste and 785 cubic yards (600 cubic meters) of low-level waste are produced.

Spent nuclear fuel from Japan arrives in Britain for reprocessing.

Radiation and Life

Radiation, which is silent, invisible, odorless, and potentially deadly, is something that we fear. Our senses give us no warning of the presence of radiation and this, perhaps, makes it even more frightening. So what does radiation actually do to living things?

Ionizing radiation

Most radiation can be divided into two groups: electromagnetic radiation, which includes radio waves, visible light, X-rays, and gamma rays; and particle radiation, such as the **neutrons, alpha particles,** and **beta particles** given off by **radioactive decay.**

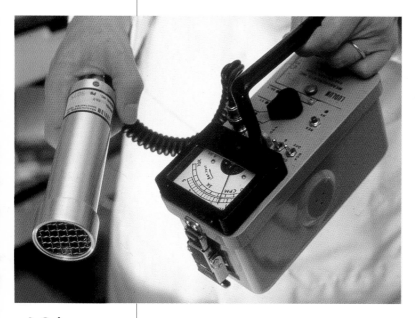

A Geiger counter is used to detect **radioactivity.**

Alpha and beta particles carry an electric charge. When alpha or beta particles pass through matter, the electrical forces between the particles and the **electrons** surrounding the **atoms** in the matter can be enough to push electrons from their orbits. This leaves the atom with a positive charge. This process is called ionization, and radiation that does this is called **ionizing radiation.**

Atoms are held together by bonds formed through sharing or transferring electrons. If electrons are removed by ionizing radiation, then these bonds are broken and new ones may be formed. If these chemical changes take place in a living organism they can bring about biological changes that could be harmful. The amount of energy needed to cause damage to a living system is extremely small. It is the ionization and the interference it causes to chemical processes that do the damage.

The effect on cells

Ionizing radiation can cause damage to any part of a living **cell**. However, damage to the cell **nucleus** tends to be more serious, because this is where the cell's DNA is found. DNA is like a chemical codebook carrying the instructions the cell needs to operate properly. If the cell's DNA is damaged, its activities are interrupted and it may no longer be able to divide. This can have terrible effects on the body's cells, such as those that line the intestines. Here, cell division takes place continually as new surface cells are made to protect cells underneath. This protection will be lost if cell division stops.

Another possibility is that a damaged cell might begin dividing uncontrollably, resulting in cancer. Sometimes the damage done to the DNA may become apparent only if the affected person has children. All of the children's cells will carry the mutation, or significant change, that has been passed on by the parent. Most mutations are harmful and result in miscarriages or life-threatening birth defects.

Cells do have ways to repair the damage caused by ionizing radiation. For example, new DNA may be made to replace damaged parts. However, the repair methods can fail if there is a sudden, very large dose of radiation, or if there are several doses separated by short periods of time.

Workers have to wear special protective radiation suits to carry out their duties.

Dosage and Damage

Workers in the potentially dangerous environment of a nuclear power plant wear a dosimeter like this to check their exposure to radiation.

The type of **radiation** damage done to living animals depends on the type of radiation involved. **Alpha particles** are given off by **elements.** The range of an alpha particle is very short. It will not go through the body tissues, and it gives up its energy rapidly. Because they cause **ionizing** over a short distance, alpha particles are said to be *densely ionizing.* Damage is concentrated in a few **cells,** and it is difficult to repair. Alpha radiation particles are a serious risk if they get inside the body, such as when uranium mine workers breathe in **radioactive** dust particles.

Beta particles are high-energy **electrons** that can more easily go through body tissues than alpha particles can. The ionizing they produce is spread over a greater distance so they are said to be *lightly ionizing.* The damage they cause can be more readily repaired.

Gamma radiation has a high capacity to pierce body tissues, but is only lightly ionizing. The ionization effect occurs only if the gamma rays strike **atoms,** causing them to send out electrons. Gamma rays are dangerous because they can pierce deep into body tissues.

Safe levels?

It is extremely difficult to define a safe level of exposure to any potentially damaging substance, let alone radioactive ones. By *safe* do we mean "no risk at all?" This is just not practical, so we have to determine instead what level of risk is acceptable. The next stage is to determine what level of radiation exposure matches the risk we are prepared to take. This is another difficult task. At lower levels of exposure, the best we can do is say that there is some chance of cancer and that risk increases with more and more exposure. What we cannot do is state with any confidence what the particular effect will be.

Working with radioactivity

Health officials want to be sure that people are not putting themselves at too much of a risk by working in nuclear power plants. Scientists have done several studies on the effects of low-level radiation exposure on workers. So far, it has not been proven that exposure to low-levels of radiation increases the chances that a worker will develop cancer. The higher levels of radiation are what workers must avoid.

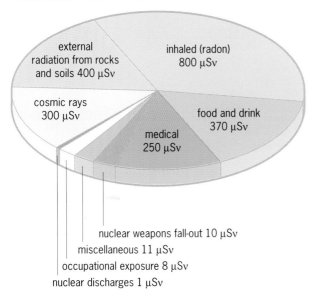

external radiation from rocks and soils 400 µSv

inhaled (radon) 800 µSv

cosmic rays 300 µSv

food and drink 370 µSv

medical 250 µSv

nuclear weapons fall-out 10 µSv
miscellaneous 11 µSv
occupational exposure 8 µSv
nuclear discharges 1 µSv

Setting the limits

Recommendations on radiation limits are set by the International Commission on Radiological Protection (ICRP). The ICRP says that no practice involving exposure to radiation should be adopted unless it produces an overall benefit to the population.

According to the ICRP, all exposures to radiation should be **a**s **l**ow **a**s **r**easonably **p**ractical (the ALARP principle). People who oppose the reprocessing of nuclear wastes claim it produces no overall benefit and therefore cannot be justified.

Radiation exposure is measured in sieverts (Sv). People can absorb 0.25 Sv without harmful effects. 1.5 Sv can produce radiation sickness. 8 Sv is fatal. This chart shows exposure levels for an average person in millionths (µ) of Sv.

Reactor Accidents

The biggest danger from nuclear power comes from exposure to **radiation.** So far, major **reactor** accidents that give off radiation into the environment have been rare. However, they have happened in the past and could happen again.

Three Mile Island

On March 28, 1979, a pump circulating cooling water in one of two pressurized water reactors at Three Mile Island in Harrisburg, Pennsylvania, stopped operating. The **coolant** immediately began to heat up, and a few seconds later a pressure-release valve opened. Seconds after this, the reactor shutdown rods automatically began working, and the **chain reaction** was stopped. Soon the coolant temperature and pressure dropped, but the pressure-release valve stayed open.

The open valve allowed water to escape from the cooling circuit. It was eventually pumped into a storage tank from which **fission** products escaped into the environment. After two minutes, the falling coolant pressure triggered the emergency core cooling system. The operators, mistakenly thinking there was too much water in the core, turned the emergency cooling system off. Eventually the water in the main cooling circuit started to boil and the **cladding** on the **fuel rods** began to melt. Workers could not reestablish adequate cooling for sixteen hours. By that time, a third of the fuel had melted, and the building had been **contaminated.** The reactor was never used again.

This is the nuclear power station at Three Mile Island in Pennsylvania.

Windscale

In 1957, a fire broke out in the reactor at Windscale, in Cumbria, Britain. So far, it is the most serious accident to have occurred in that country.

On October 1, 1957, what had been a standard procedure went wrong. The temperature rose in the reactor and both the graphite **moderator** and the uranium fuel caught on fire. **Radioactive** fission products were given off into the atmosphere. Because of this, milk from an area 193 square miles (500 square kilometers) around the location had to be destroyed to prevent people from eating or drinking anything with radioactive iodine in it. None of the workers were exposed to levels high enough to cause radiation sickness, but they, and many other people living nearby, received doses far greater than the permitted levels. A full report of the accident was not made public until 1982. At this time, the country's National Radiological Protection Board suggested that about 32 people died of cancer as a result of the contamination.

Expecting the unexpected

One problem that the mistakes at Three Mile Island made clear was that when accidents happen, workers may have no experience in dealing with them. Yet accidents in nuclear power stations can be so incredibly dangerous, it is essential that they be dealt with properly. One way to make sure this happens is to use models of reactors in training exercises. A computer connected to a control panel makes it look as if the reactor is being affected by different events. This gives the operator a chance to learn how to deal with a variety of events.

Workers at Three Mile Island practice recovering items from a model of the damaged reactor.

Chernobyl and Beyond

The worst nuclear accident to date happened on April 26, 1986, to one of the **reactors** at Chernobyl in the former Soviet Union. The Chernobyl reactor had been operating since 1984 and was one of the country's most successful nuclear power stations.

As part of a safety study, workers ran a test to determine how long the electricity generators would run if the steam supply to the **turbine** was cut off. During the test, the power level fell uncontrollably to a point where the reactor was becoming unstable. The reactor would have shut itself down immediately, but the operators prevented this. Despite the problems, they decided to go ahead with the test and shut off the steam supply to the turbines.

Out of control

At this point, only seven control rods were in the core, even though the operating instructions required at least thirty. The reactor became supercritical, and the control rods could not be inserted quickly enough to bring it under control. Within seconds, the power rose to 100 times its greatest level. Most of the core melted. A chemical explosion followed, as the melted fuel reacted with the cooling water and lifted the 2,000-ton reactor cap off. The building containing the reactor was blown apart. **Fission** products from the core were lifted high into the atmosphere by the hot gas and continued to stream out for ten days. By the time the fire was brought under control, **radioactive** material had spread across Europe.

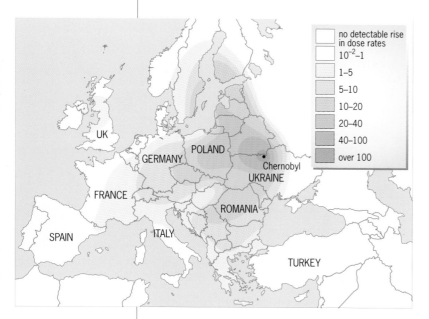

no detectable rise in dose rates
10^{-2}–1
1–5
5–10
10–20
20–40
40–100
over 100

UK
GERMANY
POLAND
Chernobyl
UKRAINE
FRANCE
ROMANIA
SPAIN
ITALY
TURKEY

Radiation levels rose across Europe after the Chernobyl disaster.

Learning from Chernobyl

Sosnovy Bor, near St. Petersburg, has a machine on the town hall building that displays local **radiation** levels in large red letters. The machine is a geiger counter, a device that can detect **alpha particles** and other **ionizing radiation.** The town's only industry is the Leningrad Nuclear Power Plant, a Chernobyl-type power station. One of the four reactors is due to be shut down because of a 1992 leak of radioactive materials. A complete reworking of the plant's safety systems, which should have been completed in 1999, has been delayed. If Chernobyl had happened there, many of the four million people of St. Petersburg would have received a huge dose of radiation.

Most experts agree that the only way to make the reactors safe is to shut them down. The U.S. Department of Energy has a list of the world's seven most dangerous reactors, and all are in what was formerly the Soviet Union. In a 1995 report, the agency explained that many Soviet-designed reactors are still potential safety risks. The reactors continue to have serious incidents, which increases the likelihood of another accident similar to the one at Chernobyl.

The damage caused by the explosion at Chernobyl is clear.

Could it happen again?

A spokesperson for the International Atomic Energy Agency was asked if he thought another Chernobyl could happen. He responded by saying, "I don't think so. Safety has improved throughout the world. But there are no guarantees. And there's absolutely no reason for complacency. We have to do our best and cross our fingers."

Nuclear Future

During the 1980s, orders for the building or starting up of nuclear **reactors** numbered between 20 to 40 per year. By comparison, by 1997, there were just two new orders and five start-ups worldwide. In 1998, construction began on only four new nuclear reactors. These were in China, Taiwan, and Japan. Money problems, not **radiation** dangers, are bringing about the end of the nuclear power industry. As nuclear power plants age, it becomes more and more expensive to maintain them. But because around sixteen percent of the world's power now comes from nuclear power plants, alternatives will have to be found.

On March 27, 2001, in a speech to the Energy and Air Quality Subcommittee of the U.S. Energy and Commerce Committee, Congressman Billy Tauzin acknowledged the role **nuclear energy** has played in the country's energy supplies. Tauzin recommended that different government agencies work together to maintain the country's nuclear energy capacity well into the future.

Out with the old: Closing nuclear plants

During the course of its nuclear weapons production and energy research, the United States built 20,000 nuclear facilities. Today, more than 5,000 of those facilities are unwanted or unused. In 1994, the U.S. Department of Energy initiated its National Decommissioning Program, which vowed to safely and economically remove these plants from service in a timely manner. In 2001, the group decided to step up its efforts.

In with the new: Working with fusion

Nuclear **fusion** is the opposite of nuclear **fission**. Nuclear fusion occurs when the **nuclei** of two lighter **atoms** combine to form a heavier one, rather than a heavy **nucleus** splitting apart. The resulting atom has a smaller **mass** than the original ones, because some of the mass is changed into energy.

This is the process that powers hydrogen bombs and stars. Gram for gram, fusion produces eight times more energy than the fission of uranium, and over a million times more than could be gained by burning the same weight of **fossil fuels.**

Fusion is not only useful because it is such a good source of energy, but also because **isotopes** of hydrogen, the fuels it uses, are fairly abundant. Also, the product of the reaction is inactive helium, rather than polluting gases or **radioactive** waste.

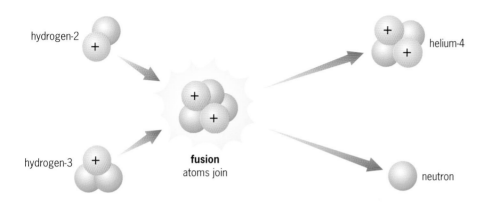

hydrogen-2

hydrogen-3

fusion
atoms join

helium-4

neutron

Two isotopes of hydrogen go through fusion to become helium plus a neutron.

Many countries, particularly the United States, Japan, and the European Union are researching controlled fusion energy. However, in experiments so far, the energy gathered in the laboratory has scarcely exceeded the energy used to run the tests. Fusion reactions are difficult to achieve because the nuclei have to be made to collide at very high speeds. This requires temperatures of 212 million° F (100 million° C) or higher.

Few people believe that fusion power will be available commercially in the foreseeable future. The extremely high cost of fusion research, and the uncertainty of the results, makes most businesses and governments reluctant to finance its development. Cooperation among countries to share the costs may be the only way to move forward.

This nuclear fusion test reactor is at Princeton University in New Jersey.

Nuclear Power, Nuclear Weapons

There is no better way to show how people's ideas can be turned to a terrible purpose than with nuclear weapons. The discovery that vast amounts of energy could be given off by splitting the **atom** was exciting because it brought a new source of power. However, the effort to harness atomic power was not caused by the desire to benefit society, but rather to produce a bomb. The successful explosion of the first atomic bomb at Los Alamos, New Mexico, on July 16, 1945, began a new era. For many years to come, the threat of nuclear destruction would hang over Earth.

A bigger bang

In conventional explosives, a chemical reaction gives off energy very quickly. The amount of energy given off depends on the **mass** of the explosive chemicals. Nuclear weapons are different. However, the amount of energy they give off is often compared to how much TNT, a common explosive, would be needed to produce the same results.

A **fission** weapon contains pure, or nearly pure, plutonium 239 or uranium enriched to over 90 percent U235. Around the outside of the bomb is a layer of common explosives. When the explosives are triggered, the **fissile material** is squeezed together, bringing about a runaway **chain reaction** within millionths of a second.

An American soldier surveys the damage caused by the atomic bomb at Hiroshima.

A **fusion** weapon uses the power of a fission bomb to provide the energy needed to heat up and squeeze **isotopes** of hydrogen so that they fuse together and give off dangerous amounts of energy. Because fusion weapons use hydrogen, they are often referred to as hydrogen bombs, or H bombs.

Weapons production

If a country wants to build nuclear weapons, it needs a supply of fissile material. It needs either a uranium enrichment facility or a nuclear **reactor** to produce plutonium and a reprocessing plant to collect it. The amount of plutonium needed to make a weapon varies, but 22 pounds (10 kilograms) is a fair average. Very small reactors, ones not designed to produce electricity, can be used to produce weapons. Without effective international controls on how nuclear fuels are reprocessed, there is always the possibility that plutonium will be mined for weapons production.

Bomb energy

The bombs dropped on Hiroshima and Nagasaki in World War II were fission bombs. The energy they gave off was the equivalent of 12,500 and 20,000 tons of dynamite respectively.

Nuclear countries

There are a number of countries that have nuclear power but do not have nuclear weapons. These include Canada, Japan, Sweden, and the Netherlands. Israel, however, has nuclear weapons but no nuclear power.

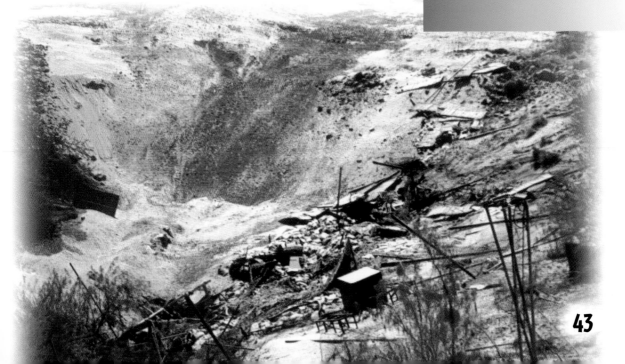

Tension between India and Pakistan grew in 1998 when India performed five underground nuclear weapons tests near the Pakistan border.

International Nuclear Event Scale

The International Nuclear Event Scale (INES) was designed to communicate to the public the safety issues of reported events at nuclear sites. There are seven levels of incidents. Level 7 is the most dangerous.

7 Major accident
A large fraction of the **radioactive** material of a large facility is given off into the environment. This can result in short-term and long-term health effects over a wide area, possibly involving more than one country. It can also have long-term effects on the environment. Example: Chernobyl, U.S.S.R. (now Ukraine), 1986.

6 Serious accident
Radiation is given off into the environment at a level that is likely to result in the activation of local emergency plans to limit serious health effects. Example: Kyshtym Reprocessing Plant, U.S.S.R. (now Russia), 1957.

5 Accident with off-site risks
Radiation is given off into the environment that is likely to result in the partial activation of local emergency plans. This type of accident can cause serious damage to the nuclear facility, such as a major accident, fire, or explosion, leading to large amounts of radiation being given off within the facility. Examples: Three Mile Island, Pennsylvania, 1979; and Windscale Pile, Great Britain, 1957.

4 Accident without significant off-site risks
Radiation is given off into the environment that results in little need for off-site actions except perhaps local food control. There may be significant damage to the nuclear facility itself, however, which would lead to major on-site recovery problems, such as a partial core melt in a power **reactor**. One or more workers may be exposed to more radiation than the acceptable levels, resulting in a high probability of a shortened life span. Examples: Windscale Reprocessing Plant, Britain, 1973; Saint-Laurent NPP, France, 1980; and Buenos Aires Critical Assembly, Argentina, 1983.

3 Serious incident
Radiation is given off into the environment that is above allowable limits, possibly affecting the health of the workers. Example: Vandellos Nuclear Power Plant, Spain, 1989.

2 Incident
Significant failure in safety provisions, an event resulting in a dose to a worker over the allowable levels, or an event that leads to significant amounts of radiation being given off within the facility. Example: Sosnovy Bor, Russia, 1992.

1 Anomaly
Event occurring beyond controlled limits due to equipment failure, human error, or faulty procedures.

Timeline

1896 French physicist Antoine Henri Becquerel discovers **radioactivity.**

1905 Albert Einstein shows that **mass** and energy can be changed from one to the other.

1919 New Zealand physicist Ernest Rutherford splits the **atom** by bombarding a nitrogen **nucleus** with **alpha particles.**

1939 Otto Hahn, Fritz Strassmann, and Lise Meitner announce the discovery of nuclear **fission.**

1942 Enrico Fermi builds the first nuclear reactor at the University of Chicago.

1945 The first atom bomb is detonated at Los Alamos, New Mexico.

1951 The Experimental Breeder Reactor in Idaho produces the first electricity generated by **nuclear energy.**

1956 The world's first commercial nuclear power station, Calder Hall, comes into operation in Britain.

1957 Spread of radiation from Windscale nuclear power station, in Cumbria, England. In Kyshtym, U.S.S.R., escape of plutonium waste caused an unknown number of casualties. On maps produced the following year, 30 small communities had been deleted.

1979 Nuclear-reactor accident at Three Mile Island, Pennsylvania happens.

1986 Explosion in a reactor at Chernobyl results in clouds of radioactive material spreading as far as Sweden.

1991 The first controlled production of nuclear-**fusion** energy is achieved at the Joint European Torus in Culham, England.

1995 Sizewell B, Britain's first pressurized water nuclear reactor and the most advanced nuclear power station in the world, begins operating in Suffolk, England.

1997 English physicists at JET produce a record 12 megawatts of nuclear-fusion power.

1999 Japan's worst-ever nuclear accident exposes 49 people, mostly plant workers, to potentially harmful levels of radiation.

Glossary

alpha particle positively charged, high-energy particle made up of two protons and two neutrons that is given off from the nucleus of a radioactive atom

atomic number number of protons in the nucleus of an atom

atom smallest unit of matter that can take part in a chemical reaction; smallest part of an element that can exist

beta particle electron sent out at high speed from the nucleus of a radioactive atom; created when a neutron changes into a proton, giving off an electron as it does so

boron chemical element used in the making of control rods for nuclear reactors because of its ability to absorb neutrons

cell smallest unit of life

chain reaction fission reaction in which neutrons given off by the splitting of atomic nuclei strike other nuclei, causing them to split and give off more neutrons, and so on

chemical energy energy in the bonds that hold atoms together in molecules that is given off during a chemical reaction

cladding metal covering on a rod or pellet of fissile material

contaminate to make impure by adding unwanted or undesirable substances

coolant chemical designed to cool something down

decay break down of the nuclei of radioactive elements

diffuse to mingle with another substance through the movement of particles

electron particle with a negative electric charge that orbits around the central nucleus of an atom

element substance that cannot be split into a simpler substance by means of a chemical reaction

fissile material element that will break apart, or fission, when struck by a neutron

fission when a large nucleus breaks down into two smaller nuclei

fossil fuel fuel produced through the action of heat and pressure on the fossil remains of plants and animals that lived millions of years ago

fuel rod rod or pellet of fissile material, usually uranium, used to power a nuclear reactor

fusion when two small nuclei combine to form a larger nucleus

gamma radiation high-energy, short-wavelength electromagnetic radiation given off from a radioactive atom

half-life time it takes for half of an amount of a radioactive substance to decay, ranging from billionths of a second to billions of years

heat energy energy created by moving atoms and molecules

ionizing radiation radiation that knocks electrons from atoms, thereby creating positively charged ions

isotope atom with the same number of protons but with a different number of neutrons

kinetic energy energy of movement

mass amount of matter in an object

meltdown accident in a nuclear reactor in which the reactor core melts as a result of the fuel overheating

moderator material used in a nuclear reactor to lower the speed of high-energy neutrons to control the rate at which energy is produced

molecule two or more atoms joined by chemical bonds; if the atoms are the same, it is an element; if they are different, it is a compound

neutron particle with no electric charge found in the central nucleus of an atom

nuclear energy energy in the nucleus of an atom given off when a large nucleus breaks into two smaller nuclei or when two small nuclei form a larger nucleus

nucleus central part of an atom, made up of protons and neutrons and containing nearly all of the atom's mass

oxide compound that contains oxygen

photon particle representing the smallest possible amount of light or other electromagnetic radiation

porous capable of having liquids and other substances pass through it

proton particle with a positive electric charge found in the central nucleus of the atom

radiation energy given off in the form of fast-moving particles or electromagnetic waves as a result of the decay of an atomic nucleus

radioactive gives off radiation

radioactivity giving off of radiation by a substance in the forms of alpha and beta particles and gamma rays

reactor structure in which radioactive material is made to break down in a controlled way, releasing energy that can be put to use

terrorist person who uses terror, such as the threat of violence, to control other people

turbine engine in which a fluid is used to spin a shaft by pushing on angled blades; used to spin electricity generators

More Books to Read

Graham, Ian. *Nuclear Power.* Austin, Tex.: Raintree Steck-Vaughn, 1999.

Oxlade, Chris. *Energy.* Chicago: Heinemann Library, 1999.

Riley, Peter. *Energy.* Chicago: Heinemann Library, 1998.

Snedden, Robert. *Energy.* Chicago: Heinemann Library, 1999.

Index